S0-BON-829

This book belongs to:

Family HAAS

Sep 4 / 95

PROVERBS
for
TODAY

INSPIRATIONAL KEEPSAKES
FROM LONGMEADOW PRESS:

Proverbs for Today

Psalms for Today

Reflections from Jesus

Passages for Consolation

PROVERBS
for
TODAY

Edited by Michael Myers

LONGMEADOW PRESS

Jacket design by Lisa Amoroso
Interior design by Lisa Amoroso
ISBN: 0-681-41442-1
Printed in U.S.A.
First Edition
0 9 8 7 6 5 4 3 2 1

Wisdom

The proverbs of Solomon the son of David, king of Israel;

To know wisdom and instruction; to perceive the words of understanding;

To receive the instruction of wisdom, justice, and judgment, and equity;

To give subtilty to the simple, to the young man knowledge and discretion.

A wise *man* will hear, and will increase learning; and a man of understanding shall attain unto wise counsels.

Proverbs 1:1–5

Hatred stirreth up strifes: but love covereth all sins.

Proverbs 10:12

But the path of the just *is* as the shining light,
that shineth more and more unto the perfect day.

Proverbs 4:18

Happy *is* the man *that* findeth wisdom, and the
man *that* getteth understanding.

For the merchandise of it *is* better than the
merchandise of silver, and the gain thereof than
fine gold.

She *is* more precious than rubies: and all the
things thou canst desire are not to be compared
unto her.

Proverbs 3:13–15

As a jewel of gold in a swine's snout, *so is* a fair woman which is without discretion.

Proverbs 11:22

Receive my instruction, and not silver; and knowledge rather than choice gold.

For wisdom *is* better than rubies; and all the things that may be desired are not to be compared to it.

Proverbs 8:10, 11

Wisdom *is* the principal thing; *therefore* get wisdom: and with all thy getting get understanding.

Proverbs 4:7

The LORD by wisdom hath founded the earth; by understanding hath he established the heavens.

By his knowledge the depths are broken up, and the clouds drop down the dew.

My son, let not them depart from thine eyes: keep sound wisdom and discretion:

So shall they be life unto thy soul, and grace to thy neck.

Then shalt thou walk in thy way safely, and thy foot shall not stumble.

When thou liest down, thou shalt not be afraid: yea, thou shalt lie down, and thy sleep shall be sweet.

Proverbs 3:19–24

My son, if thou wilt receive my words, and hide my commandments with thee;

So that thou incline thine ear unto wisdom, *and* apply thine heart to understanding;

Yea, if thou criest after knowledge, *and* liftest up thy voice for understanding;

If thou seekest her as silver, and searchest for her as *for* hid treasures;

Then shalt thou understand the fear of the LORD, and find the knowledge of God.

For the LORD giveth wisdom: out of his mouth *cometh* knowledge and understanding.

Proverbs 2:1–6

He becometh poor that dealeth *with* a slack
hand: but the hand of the diligent maketh rich.

Proverbs 10:4

The blessing of the LORD, it maketh rich, and he
addeth no sorrow with it.

Proverbs 10:22

Behold, the righteous shall be recompensed in
the earth: much more the wicked and the sinner.

Proverbs 11:31

The wicked are overthrown, and *are* not: but the house of the righteous shall stand.

Proverbs 12:7

Lying lips *are* abomination to the LORD: but they that deal truly *are* his delight.

Proverbs 12:22

Only by pride cometh contention: but with the well advised *is* wisdom.

Proverbs 13:10

The desire accomplished is sweet to the soul: but *it is* abomination to fools to depart from evil.

Proverbs 13:19

The wicked is snared by the transgression of *his* lips: but the just shall come out of trouble.

Proverbs 12:13

There is that maketh himself rich, yet *hath* nothing: *there is* that maketh himself poor, yet *hath* great riches.

Proverbs 13:7

Hope deferred maketh the heart sick: but *when* the desire cometh, *it is* a tree of life.

Proverbs 13:12

Every wise woman buildeth her house: but the foolish plucketh it down with her hands.

Proverbs 14:1

The simple believeth every word: but the prudent *man* looketh well to his going.

Proverbs 14:15

A faithful witness will not lie: but a false witness will utter lies.

Proverbs 14:5

He that oppresseth the poor reproacheth his Maker: but he that honoureth him hath mercy on the poor.

Proverbs 14:31

The heart of the righteous studieth to answer: but the mouth of the wicked poureth out evil things.

Proverbs 15:28

A sound heart *is* the life of the flesh: but envy the rottenness of the bones.

Proverbs 14:30

Folly *is* joy to *him that is* destitute of wisdom: but a man of understanding walketh uprightly.

Proverbs 15:21

The fear of the LORD *is* the instruction of wisdom; and before honour *is* humility.

Proverbs 15:33

All the ways of a man *are* clean in his own eyes; but the LORD weigheth the spirits.

Proverbs 16:2

When a man's ways please the LORD, he maketh even his enemies to be at peace with him.

Proverbs 16:7

A man's heart deviseth his way: but the LORD directeth his steps.

Proverbs 16:9

Pride *goeth* before destruction, and an haughty spirit before a fall.

Proverbs 16:18

Every one *that* is proud in heart *is* an abomination to the LORD: *though* hand *join* in hand, he shall not be unpunished.

Proverbs 16:5

Righteous lips *are* the delight of kings; and they love him that speaketh right.

Proverbs 16:13

Better *is* a little with righteousness than great revenues without right.

Proverbs 16:8

A just weight and balance *are* the LORD's: all the weights of the bag *are* his work.

Proverbs 16:11

How much better *is it* to get wisdom than gold! and to get understanding rather to be chosen than silver!

Proverbs 16:16

He that handleth a matter wisely shall find
good: and whoso trusteth in the LORD, happy *is* he.

Proverbs 16:20

Better *is* a dry morsel, and quietness therewith,
than an house full of sacrifices *with* strife.

Proverbs 17:1

Children's children *are* the crown of old men;
and the glory of children *are* their fathers.

Proverbs 17:6

He that hath knowledge spareth his words: *and* a man of understanding is of an excellent spirit.

Proverbs 17:27

He also that is slothful in his work is brother to him that is a great waster.

Proverbs 18:9

The heart of the prudent getteth knowledge; and the ear of the wise seeketh knowledge.

Proverbs 18:15

Whoso findeth a wife findeth a good *thing*, and obtaineth favour of the LORD.

Proverbs 18:22

The fining pot *is* for silver, and the furnace for gold: but the LORD trieth the hearts.

Proverbs 17:3

Excellent speech becometh not a fool: much less do lying lips a prince.

Proverbs 17:7

The words of a man's mouth *are as* deep waters,
and the wellspring of wisdom *as* a flowing brook.

Proverbs 18:4

The name of the LORD *is* a strong tower: the
righteous runneth into it, and is safe.

Proverbs 18:10

A man's gift maketh room for him, and bringeth
him before great men.

Proverbs 18:16

A man *that hath* friends must shew himself friendly: and there is a friend *that* sticketh closer than a brother.

Proverbs 18:24

Also, *that* the soul *be* without knowledge, *it is* not good; and he that hasteth with *his* feet sinneth.

Proverbs 19:2

A false witness shall not be unpunished, and *he that* speaketh lies shall not escape.

Proverbs 19:5

He that wasteth *his* father, *and* chaseth away *his* mother, *is* a son that causeth shame, and bringeth reproach.

Proverbs 19:26

Most men will proclaim every one his own goodness: but a faithful man who can find?

Proverbs 20:6

Love not sleep, lest thou come to poverty; open thine eyes, *and* thou shall be satisfied with bread.

Proverbs 20:13

Wealth maketh many friends; but the poor is separated from his neighbour.

Proverbs 19:4

Many will intreat the favour of the prince: and every man *is* a friend to him that giveth gifts.

Proverbs 19:6

The glory of young men *is* their strength: and the beauty of old men *is* the grey head.

Proverbs 20:29

Counsel in the heart of man *is like* deep water;
but a man of understanding will draw it out.

Proverbs 20:5

Even a child is known by his doings, whether
his work *be* pure, and whether *it be* right.

Proverbs 20:11

Bread of deceit *is* sweet to a man; but afterwards
his mouth shall be filled with gravel.

Proverbs 20:17

To do justice and judgment *is* more acceptable to the LORD than sacrifice.

Proverbs 21:3

Whoso stoppeth his ears at the cry of the poor, he also shall cry himself, but shall not be heard.

Proverbs 21:13

A *good* name *is* rather to be chosen than great riches, *and* loving favour rather than silver and gold.

Proverbs 22:1

A prudent *man* foreseeth the evil, and hideth himself: but the simple pass on, and are punished.

Proverbs 22:3

Wilt thou set thine eyes upon that which is not? for *riches* certainly make themselves wings; they fly away as an eagle toward heaven.

Proverbs 23:5

The father of the righteous shall greatly rejoice: and he that begetteth a wise *child* shall have joy of him.

Proverbs 23:24

And by knowledge shall the chambers be filled with all precious and pleasant riches.

Proverbs 24:4

It is better to dwell in a corner of the housetop, than with a brawling woman and in a wide house.

Proverbs 21:9

There is no wisdom nor understanding nor counsel against the LORD.

Proverbs 21:30

The rich and poor meet together: the LORD *is* the maker of them all.

Proverbs 22:2

Seest thou a man diligent in his business? he shall stand before kings; he shall not stand before mean *men*.

Proverbs 22:29

For the drunkard and the glutton shall come to poverty: and drowsiness shall clothe *a man* with rags.

Proverbs 23:21

I went by the field of the slothful, and by the vineyard of the man void of understanding;

And, lo, it was all grown over with thorns, *and* nettles had covered the face therefore, and the stone wall thereof was broken down.

Then I saw, *and* considered *it* well: I looked upon *it*, *and* received instruction.

Yet a little sleep, a little slumber, a little folding of the hands to sleep:

So shall thy poverty come *as* one that travelleth; and thy want as an armed man.

Proverbs 24:30–34

Through wisdom is an house builded; and by understanding it is established.

Proverbs 24:3

As an earring of gold, and an ornament of fine gold, *so is* a wise reprover upon an obedient ear.

Proverbs 25:12

As cold waters to a thirsty soul, so *is* good news from a far country.

Proverbs 25:25

As a dog returneth to his vomit, *so* a fool returneth to his folly.

Proverbs 26:11

The sluggard *is* wiser in his own conceit than seven men that can render a reason.

Proverbs 26:16

As a mad *man* who casteth firebrands, arrows, and death.

Proverbs 26:18

A word fitly spoken *is like* apples of gold in pictures of silver.

Proverbs 25:11

By long forbearing is a prince persuaded, and a soft tongue breaketh the bone.

Proverbs 25:15

He that *hath* no rule over his own spirit *is like* a city *that is* broken down, *and* without walls.

Proverbs 25:28

Seest thou a man wise in his own conceit? *there is* more hope of a fool than of him.

Proverbs 26:12

He that passeth by, *and* meddleth with strife *belonging* not to him, *is like* one that taketh a dog by the ears.

Proverbs 26:17

So *is* the man *that* deceiveth his neighbour, and saith, Am not I in sport?

Proverbs 26:19

Iron sharpeneth iron; so a man sharpeneth the countenance of his friend.

Proverbs 27:17

Better *is* the poor that walketh in his uprightness, than *he that is* perverse *in his* ways, though he *be* rich.

Proverbs 28:6

Open rebuke *is* better than secret love.

Proverbs 27:5

As a roaring lion, and a ranging bear; *so is* a wicked ruler over the poor people.

Proverbs 28:15

He that hasteth to be rich *hath* an evil eye, and considereth not that poverty shall come upon him.

Proverbs 28:22

When the wicked rise, men hide themselves: but when they perish, the righteous increase.

Proverbs 28:28

Faithful *are* the wounds of a friend; but the kisses of an enemy *are* deceitful.

Proverbs 27:6

For riches *are* not for ever: and doth the crown *endure* to every generation?

Proverbs 27:24

The rich man *is* wise in his own conceit: but the poor that hath understanding searcheth him out.

Proverbs 28:11

A faithful man shall abound with blessings: but he that maketh haste to be rich shall not be innocent.

Proverbs 28:20

He that is of a proud heart stirreth up strife: but he that putteth his trust in the LORD shall be made fat.

Proverbs 28:25

When the righteous are in authority, the people rejoice: but when the wicked beareth rule, the people mourn.

Proverbs 29:2

Where *there is* no vision, the people perish: but he that keepeth the law, happy *is* he.

Proverbs 29:18

A man's pride shall bring him low: but honour shall uphold the humble in spirit.

Proverbs 29:23

If a wise man contendeth with a foolish man, whether he rage or laugh, *there is* no rest.

Proverbs 29:9

Seest thou a man *that is* hasty in his words? *there is* more hope of a fool than of him.

Proverbs 29:20

The fear of man bringeth a snare: but whoso putteth his trust in the LORD shall be safe.

Proverbs 29:25

That which is crooked cannot be made straight: and that which is wanting cannot be numbered.

Ecclesiastes 1:15

And whatsoever mine eyes desired I kept not from them, I withheld not my heart from any joy; for my heart rejoiced in all my labour: and this was my portion of all my labour.

Then I looked on all the works that my hands had wrought, and on the labour that I had laboured to do: and, behold, all *was* vanity and vexation of spirit, and *there was* no profit under the sun.

Then I saw that wisdom excelleth folly, as far as light excelleth darkness.

Then said I in my heart, As it happeneth to the fool, so it happeneth even to me; and why was I then more wise? Then I said in my heart, that this also *is* vanity.

Ecclesiastes 2:10, 11, 13, 15

There is nothing better for a man, *than* that he should eat and drink, and *that* he should make his soul enjoy good in his labour. This also I saw, that it *was* from the hand of God.

Ecclesiastes 2:24

Better *is* a poor and a wise child than an old and foolish king, who will no more be admonished.

Ecclesiastes 4:13

He that loveth silver shall not be satisfied with silver; nor he that loveth abundance with increase: this *is* also vanity.

Ecclesiastes 5:10

Two *are* better than one; because they have a good reward for their labour.

For if they fall, the one will lift up his fellow: but woe to him *that* is alone when he falleth; for *he hath* not another to help him up.

Again, if two lie together, then they have heat: but how can one be warm *alone*?

And if one prevail against him, two shall withstand him; and a threefold cord is not quickly broken.

Ecclesiastes 4:9–12

Better *is it* that thou shouldest not vow, than that thou shouldest vow and not pay.

Ecclesiastes 5:5

The sleep of a labouring man *is* sweet, whether he eat little or much: but the abundance of the rich will not suffer him to sleep.

Ecclesiastes 5:12

A good name *is* better than precious ointment; and the day of death than the day of one's birth.

Ecclesiastes 7:1

As he came forth of his mother's womb, naked shall he return to go as he came, and shall take nothing of his labour, which he may carry away in his hand.

Ecclesiastes 5:15

Counsel

My son, forget not my law; but let thine heart keep my commandments:

For length of days, and long life, and peace, shall they add to thee.

Let not mercy and truth forsake thee: bind them about thy neck; write them upon the table of thine heart:

So shalt thou find favour and good understanding in the sight of God and man.

Trust in the LORD with all thine heart; and lean not unto thine own understanding.

Proverbs 3:1–5

Strive not with a man without cause, if he have done thee no harm.

Proverbs 3:30

These six *things* doth the LORD hate: yea, seven *are* an abomination unto him:

A proud look, a lying tongue, and hands that shed innocent blood,

An heart that deviseth wicked imaginations, feet that be swift in running to mischief,

A false witness *that* speaketh lies, and he that soweth discord among brethren.

Proverbs 6:16–19

Drink waters out of thine own cistern, and running waters out of thine own well.

Let thy fountain be blessed: and rejoice with the wife of thy youth.

Let her be as the loving hind and pleasant roe; let her breasts satisfy thee at all times; and be thou ravished always with her love.

Proverbs 5:15, 18, 19

Hear instruction, and be wise, and refuse it not.

Proverbs 8:33

Let thine eyes look right on, and let thine eyelids look straight before thee.

Ponder the path of thy feet, and let all thy ways be established.

Proverbs 4:25, 26

Give *instruction* to a wise *man*, and he will be yet wiser: teach a just *man*, and he will increase in learning.

Proverbs 9:9

The way of a fool *is* right in his own eyes: but he that hearkeneth unto counsel *is* wise.

Proverbs 12:15

Wealth *gotten* by vanity shall be diminished: but he that gathereth by labour shall increase.

Proverbs 13:11

He that is slow to wrath *is* of great understanding: but *he that is* hasty of spirit exalteth folly.

Proverbs 14:29

He that diligently seeketh good procureth favour: but he that seeketh mischief, it shall come unto him.

He that trusteth in his riches shall fall: but the righteous shall flourish as a branch.

He that troubleth his own house shall inherit the wind: and the fool *shall be* servant to the wise of heart.

Proverbs 11:27–29

He that keepeth his mouth keepeth his life: *but* he that openeth wide his lips shall have destruction.

Proverbs 13:3

He that walketh with wise *men* shall be wise: but a companion of fools shall be destroyed.

Proverbs 13:20

A SOFT answer turneth away wrath: but grievous words stir up anger.

Proverbs 15:1

A wise son maketh a glad father: but a foolish man despiseth his mother.

Proverbs 15:20

A man hath joy by the answer of his mouth: and a word *spoken* in due season, how good *is it!*

Proverbs 15:23

There is a way that seemeth right unto a man, but the end thereof *are* the ways of death.

Proverbs 16:25

Better *is* a dinner of herbs where love is, than a stalled ox and hatred therewith.

Proverbs 15:17

Without counsel purposes are disappointed: but in the multitude of counsellors they are established.

Proverbs 15:22

The LORD will destroy the house of the proud: but he will establish the border of the widow.

Proverbs 15:25

He that is slow to anger *is* better than the mighty; and he that ruleth his spirit than he that taketh a city.

Proverbs 16:32

A merry heart doeth good *like* a medicine: but broken spirit drieth the bones.

Proverbs 17:22

He that answereth a matter before he heareth *it*, it *is* folly and shame unto him.

Proverbs 18:13

Death and life *are* in the power of the tongue: and they that love it shall eat the fruit thereof.

Proverbs 18:21

He that goeth about *as* a talebearer revealeth secrets: therefore meddle not with him that flattereth with his lips.

Proverbs 20:19

He that followeth after righteousness and mercy findeth life, righteousness, and honour.

Proverbs 21:21

Rob not the poor, because he *is* poor: neither oppress the afflicted in the gate.

Proverbs 22:22

Even a fool, when he holdeth his peace, is counted wise: *and* he that shutteth his lips *is esteemed* as a man of understanding.

Proverbs 17:28

He that is first in his own cause *seemeth* just; but his neighbour cometh and searcheth him.

Proverbs 18:17

Hear counsel, and receive instruction, that thou mayest be wise in thy latter end.

Proverbs 19:20

Say not thou, I will recompense evil; *but* wait on the LORD, and he shall save thee.

Proverbs 20:22

Train up a child in the way he should go: and when he is old, he will not depart from it.

Proverbs 22:6

Eat thou not the bread of *him that hath* an evil eye, neither desire thou his dainty meats.

Proverbs 23:6

Hearken unto thy father that begat thee, and despise not thy mother when she is old.

Proverbs 23:22

Be not thou envious against evil men, neither desire to be with them.

Proverbs 24:1

For by wise counsel thou shalt make thy war: and in multitude of counsellors *there is* safety.

Proverbs 24:6

Say not, I will do so to him as he hath done to me: I will render to the man according to his work.

Proverbs 24:29

Put not forth thyself in the presence of the king, and stand not in the place of great *men*:

Proverbs 25:6

Speak not in the ears of a fool: for he will despise the wisdom of thy words.

Proverbs 23:9